NIKOLA
TESLA
PHYSICIST, INVENTOR, ELECTRICAL ENGINEER

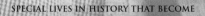

SPECIAL LIVES IN HISTORY THAT BECOME

Signature LIVES

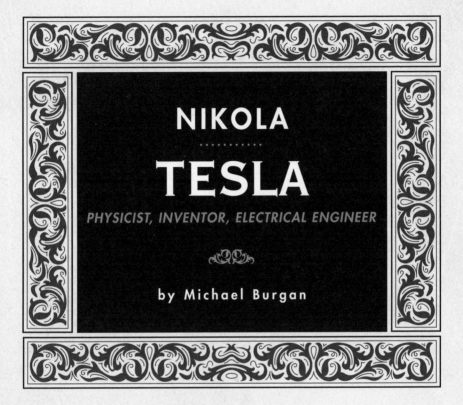

NIKOLA

TESLA

PHYSICIST, INVENTOR, ELECTRICAL ENGINEER

by Michael Burgan

Content Adviser: William H. Terbo,
Grandnephew of Nikola Tesla
and Chairman of the Executive Board,
Tesla Memorial Society Inc.

Reading Adviser: Alexa Sandmann, Ed.D.,
Professor of Literacy, College and Graduate School
of Education, Health, and Human Services,
Kent State University

Compass Point Books ✦ Minneapolis, Minnesota

Compass Point Books
151 Good Counsel Drive
P.O. Box 669
Mankato, MN 56001

This book was manufactured with paper containing at least
10 percent post-consumer waste.

Managing Editor: Catherine Neitge
Page Production: Bobbie Nuytten
Photo Researchers: Eric Gohl and Wanda Winch
Cartographer: XNR Productions, Inc.
Library Consultant: Kathleen Baxter

Art Director: LuAnn Ascheman-Adams
Creative Director: Joe Ewest
Editorial Director: Nick Healy

Library of Congress Cataloging-in-Publication Data
Burgan, Michael.
  Nikola Tesla : physicist, inventor, electrical engineer / by Michael Burgan.
    p. cm. — (Signature lives)
  Includes bibliographical references and index.
  ISBN 978-0-7565-4086-9 (library binding)
1. Tesla, Nikola, 1856–1943—Juvenile literature. 2. Electric engineers—
United States—Biography—Juvenile literature. 3. Inventors—United
States—Biography—Juvenile literature. I. Title. II. Series.
  TK140.T4B87 2009
  621.3092—dc22   [B]   2008035725

Visit Compass Point Books on the Internet at *www.compasspointbooks.com*
or e-mail your request to *custserv@compasspointbooks.com*

Signature Lives

MODERN AMERICA

Life in the United States since the late 19th century has undergone incredible changes. Advancements in technology and in society itself have transformed the lives of Americans. As they adjusted to this modern era, people cast aside old ways and embraced new ideas. The once silenced members of society—women, minorities, and young people—made their voices heard. Modern Americans survived wars, economic depression, protests, and scandals to emerge strong and ready to face whatever the future holds.

Table of Contents

Chapter

1 POWER FROM NATURE

ৎᷛ⊷⊷ᷛ৵

Nikola Tesla walked near the rushing waters of Niagara Falls, New York. His raincoat protected him from the spray that filled the air as the water roared over the rocks. On this visit in July 1896, several other men joined Tesla. Unlike most people who came to Niagara Falls, however, Tesla's group was there for business, not sightseeing.

This was Tesla's first trip to the site, but the 184-foot-high (56 meter) falls and the power in their water had interested him for decades. As a teenager in Gospic, Austrian Croatia, Nikola Tesla had seen a picture of the mighty falls. He later wrote, "I was fascinated … and pictured in my imagination a big wheel run by the falls. I told my uncle I would go to America and carry out this scheme." With the wheel,

Serbian-American inventor Nikola Tesla is known as the father of alternating current electrical systems and the inventor of radio.

For several centuries before Nikola Tesla, people who saw the rushing waters of Niagara Falls dreamed of using it as a source of power. At the top of the falls, the water held what's called potential energy—energy that is "stored." As the water falls, the potential energy becomes kinetic, or moving, energy. The rushing water that moved through the Niagara power plant also had kinetic energy, which it transferred to the turbines. This created mechanical energy. The spinning turbines then created electrical energy in the plant's generators. Energy is never lost; it simply takes a different form or moves to a different place. In his work, Tesla often studied the many forms of energy in the universe.

the young Tesla knew, the energy in the falls could be used to power machines.

Since his childhood, Tesla had had a vivid imagination. He also had worked hard to pursue his dreams of inventing useful machines and understanding the universe. Tesla did not make a big wheel to harness the power of Niagara Falls. He had, however, created a series of inventions during the 1880s that had been put to use at the falls. With his work, Tesla helped make history.

Several years before Tesla's visit to Niagara Falls, work had begun on a power plant at the site. Water from the Niagara River was sent into a newly dug canal along the shore. Water flowed through the canal and underground. Along the canal, workers constructed a building 500 feet (152.5 m) long. It held huge generators, which were connected by steel shafts to turbines below the ground. Each generator, also called a dynamo, was almost 12 feet (3.6 m) tall and just as wide.

Water from a tunnel streamed past the turbines, turning them at a rate of 250 revolutions per minute. The spinning turbines turned the shafts attached to them, and the movement of the shafts powered the generators, which then created electricity. The water used to start the process returned to the river through a tunnel. The plant at Niagara Falls was one

A scientist of Tesla's era said the amount of water that fell over Niagara Falls in one second equaled the energy stored in all the coal mined in the world in one day.

of the world's first hydroelectric power plants. It used water to create electric power. (*Hydro* comes from a Greek word meaning "water.")

As a young inventor—first in Budapest, Hungary, and then in New York—Tesla had designed all the parts needed to transmit electricity over long distances. His system used alternating current (AC). It slowly replaced the direct current (DC) system that had been popular in the United States before he reached its shores. Now, with the Niagara power plant, AC electricity flowed along wires from the generators to customers. Tesla's ideas had made possible this massive plant and its creation of electricity.

The plant had first produced power about a year before Tesla's visit. *The New York Times* told its readers that Niagara Falls was now "tak[ing] a share of the work in the world, while not losing a bit of its natural beauty." Buffalo, about 15 miles (24 kilometers) away, would soon receive Niagara energy. In years to come the falls would power electric lights in New York City, about 400 miles (644 km) away.

At the time of Tesla's trip in July 1896, he was already famous for his work with electricity, especially AC motors and generators. Reporters greeted him after he explored the power plant at Niagara Falls. The plant was "all and more than I anticipated it would be," Tesla told them:

It is fully all that was promised. It is one of the wonders of the century. ... The plant and the prospect of future development in electrical science, and the more ordinary uses of electricity, are my ideals.

Tesla continued to explore electricity and other forms of energy. He hoped to create a system that would send electricity long distances without wires. That work led him to create small remote-controlled ships powered by batteries. Tesla called these and other remotely operated vehicles "the first of a race of robots, mechanical men which will do the laborious

In a double-exposure photo, Tesla appears to be sitting in front of his magnifying transformer called the Tesla coil. It created very powerful electrical fields.

[hard] work of the human race." Later he claimed he had invented a new form of energy that could be used as a weapon. Newspapers called it a death ray, and people wondered whether it would, as Tesla claimed, end war. The inventor believed it would be used only for defense. He thought that countries that owned such a powerful weapon would never have to fear an enemy attack.

Tesla hoped the world would find peace and riches through his inventions. Even with his great intelligence, he had trouble finding either of those in his own life. He fought long legal battles with men and companies that tried to use his ideas without paying for them. Others took credit for things he invented and made his work seem unimportant. When Tesla did make money for his work, he spent it quickly and often found himself in debt. He always claimed he would create great new things if he only had enough money. After a time, investors lost faith in him, and in later years he struggled to continue his projects.

For a time Tesla was compared to the great scientists and inventors of his day, such as Thomas Edison and Guglielmo Marconi. Edison, who created the first practical incandescent lightbulb, was Tesla's rival in the field of electric power. Marconi took credit for inventing wireless radio—credit Tesla thought he deserved. Both of those men, and other great scien-

Nikola Tesla in his office about 1910; he was given a rare honor after his death—an international electrical unit, the tesla, was named after him.

tists and engineers of Tesla's era, remained famous throughout the 20th century. Tesla, though, was forgotten for a time. His achievements were ignored in many history books.

In the last few decades, however, historians have begun to write more about Tesla. He has regained some of the fame he once had as the father of AC electrical systems, the true inventor of radio, and the creator of many other important ideas about energy. Scientists are still exploring some of the ideas he first discussed long ago. ✍

2 INVENTIVE BOYHOOD

Chapter

ෙන්

If Milutin and Djouka Tesla had gotten their wish, the world might never have learned of the genius of their son Nikola. Early in the boy's life, the Teslas wanted Nikola to become a priest. Nikola resisted them and instead started down the path of science and invention.

The Teslas lived in the small mountain village of Smiljan in Austrian Croatia. The family had moved there just a year or so before Nikola was born July 10, 1856. Some sources say he was born at midnight, and Nikola never knew which day to celebrate as his birthday. He was the fourth of five children and the family's second and last son. Nikola's father, Milutin, was a Serbian Orthodox priest and had been sent to Smiljan by his church. The Serbian Orthodox religion

A monument marking the 150th anniversary of Nikola Tesla's birth was dedicated in 2006 in his hometown of Smiljan, Croatia.

traces its roots to the Eastern Orthodox faith, which had emerged from the first Christian church in the 11th century. Unlike Roman Catholic priests, Orthodox priests are allowed to marry and have families.

Although living in Austrian Croatia, both of Nikola's parents came from Serbian families. Nikola's Serbian relatives included other priests and several military officers honored for their bravery. For educated Serbians of the day, these were two of the most respected professions. They provided access to continued and advanced education.

The Croatian government restored Nikola Tesla's family home in Smiljan and the church where his father served as priest.

The Tesla family lived next to the church, far away from most of the village. The family had servants

to help with chores around their farm, which included cows and chickens. Tesla's mother worked almost nonstop each day, taking care of her children, making the family's clothes, and running the farm, while her husband handled church affairs.

A dedicated reader, Tesla's father owned a large library, and Niko, as his son was called, developed a love of books as well. He sometimes wanted to read late into the night, but his father disapproved and took away the candles the boy used. The Reverend Tesla feared his son would ruin his eyes reading by such weak light. A determined Niko then began secretly making his own candles. He blocked up the cracks around the bedroom door so the candlelight would not escape. Then, as he later wrote, he would "read, often till dawn, when all others slept."

Niko had an early interest in both inventing and electricity. He credited his mother with stirring

At the time of Nikola Tesla's birth, Serbia and Croatia were part of the huge Austro-Hungarian Empire. In 1878, Serbia gained its independence from the empire, which was later broken apart after the end of World War I. At that time, Croatia and Serbia became part of a new country, which was eventually called Yugoslavia. During the 1990s, Yugoslavia began separating into several independent countries, including Croatia and Serbia. For a time the two countries fought each other. Today both nations unite in honoring Tesla's ties to them. Tesla's childhood home in Smiljan was rebuilt and is now part of the Nikola Tesla Memorial Center. Belgrade, the capital of Serbia, is the home of the Nikola Tesla Museum, where his personal papers are stored.

his interest in creating things. Both her father and grandfather had invented as a hobby, and Djouka Tesla created tools to make her life easier around the house, including a mechanical eggbeater. She had never learned to read, but she memorized long sections of the Bible and other books, especially poems written in Serbian. Her son later shared that love of poetry. Like his wife, the Reverend Tesla had a strong memory. He made Niko memorize parts of books so he, too, would develop his mind and learn to remember facts of all kinds.

Niko's first attempt at inventing was simple—making a hook out of wire and attaching it to string. He used the tool to catch frogs. Next he made a small propeller that was powered by June bugs. The young

Tesla's bedroom in his restored family home

inventor glued four live bugs to each of four blades, and the bugs' moving wings made the propeller turn. The invention, however, came to an unexpected end. The son of a visiting military officer enjoyed eating insects, and he pulled the June bugs off the blades and ate them. The sight, Tesla later wrote, ended his efforts with bugs, "and I have never since been able to touch a Maybug [June bug] or any other insect for that matter."

The young inventor often thought about flying, and he imagined himself soaring freely through the skies. He tried to turn the image into reality with the help of an umbrella. He went to the top of a barn, opened the umbrella, and jumped. Niko had thought the umbrella would work like a parachute and carry him gently to the ground. Instead the boy fell with a thud, hitting his head and knocking himself out. His mother found him on the ground and carried him home.

Niko's first encounter with electricity came with the family cat, Macak (the Serbian word for cat). One winter night, as he stroked the cat's fur, Niko saw "a sheet of light and my hand produced a shower of erupting sparks loud enough to be heard all over the place." His father explained that the light and noise were a kind of electricity. In that instant Niko became fascinated by electricity and wanted to know more about it.

Niko began his schooling when he was 5. The

The electricity created when Nikola Tesla petted his cat was static electricity. It generally occurs when the air is very dry, such as in winter. Static electricity is created when the atoms of a material have a buildup of tiny particles called electrons. Atoms can have a positive or negative charge, depending on how many electrons they have in relation to other tiny particles within atoms, called protons. An atom is negatively charged when it has more electrons than protons and is positively charged when it has more protons than electrons. With Tesla's cat, the atoms in its fur had a positive charge, while his hand had a negative charge. Electrons in the fur jumped to his hand, creating the static electricity.

next year, the Teslas moved to the nearby town of Gospic, where Niko went to elementary school. He missed the simple farm life of Smiljan, but he generally did well in school. He built his first model of a water turbine during this time. He also won praise for solving a problem in the city. During a test of a new fire engine, no water came out of the hose. The source for the water was a nearby river. Niko waded into the water and saw that the hose feeding the fire engine had collapsed. He fixed it, and the engine quickly shot out water, soaking some of the people nearby. No one seemed to mind, though, as they carried young Niko on their shoulders, treating him like a hero.

Niko's boyhood was filled with fun, adventure, and learning, but one sad incident deeply affected him and the family. When Niko was about 7, his older brother Dane fell off the family horse and died. Niko saw the horrible accident and never forgot the sight. He also knew how much Dane's death upset his parents, who considered him their most gifted child. Anything Niko accomplished, he later wrote, "merely caused my parents to feel their loss [of Dane] more keenly. So I grew up with little confidence in myself."

At least one historian has wondered whether Dane's death triggered several problems that Tesla had throughout his life. He developed strange dislikes and patterns of behavior. For example, he could not stand to see women wearing earrings, and he hated

Austrian Croatia was part of Austria-Hungary, an empire that stretched through central Europe. The empire lasted from 1867 to 1918.

Map shows boundaries of 1871.

touching other people's hair. He also later claimed, "I would get a fever by looking at a peach."

Shortly after his brother's death, Niko found a novel in his father's library. The book talked about having willpower and self-control, and the boy eagerly accepted those ideas. From then on, he wrote:

> *I began to discipline myself. Had I a sweet cake or a juicy apple which I was dying to eat I would give it to another boy … pained but satisfied. Had I some difficult task before me which was exhausting I would attack it again and again until it was done.*

Perhaps Niko's desire to control himself and do well was meant to make up for the family's loss of his brother. Whatever the reason, the adult Tesla believed those behaviors led to his success as an inventor.

At 10 Niko entered the local *real gymnasium,* which was similar to a middle school. He was fascinated with math and science and showed great skill in them. He already had the ability to visualize scenes of places he had never been and people he had never seen. That talent of seeing things so clearly in his mind helped Niko do math problems without writing them down. In years to come this ability to visualize helped him "see" his inventions before he made them.

When he finished his studies in Gospic, Niko

moved to Karlovac, Austrian Croatia. Living with an aunt there, he attended a high school and spent even more time studying science and learning all he could about electricity. Niko ached to become an electrical engineer, but he knew his father wanted him to become a priest.

When his schooling in Karlovac ended, Niko reluctantly planned to follow his father's wishes. Then an illness changed his future. Going back to Gospic, Niko was struck with cholera, a serious stomach ailment. He seemed close to death, and he said to his father, "Perhaps I may get well if you will let me study engineering." The elder Tesla agreed that if Niko recovered, he would not have to become a priest. Soon Niko recovered, and his father kept his promise. Niko would study science. 🕭

3 THE FIRST GREAT DISCOVERY

Before heading off to college, Nikola Tesla spent a year roaming the mountainsides of Austrian Croatia. In his brief autobiography, *My Inventions* (written in 1919), Tesla says the stay in the mountains was meant to help him regain his strength after his almost-deadly bout of cholera. Recent historians, however, think the hiking expedition had another purpose. At the time the Austro-Hungarian Empire forced all young men to serve in the military for three years. The Reverend Tesla did not want his son to serve, so he sent him away so local officials could not find him. Tesla's relatives in the military may have also used their influence to help keep him out of the army. In addition, most college students did not have to serve in the military.

At the urging of his father, Tesla eventually attended college in Prague, in what is now the Czech Republic. But he lasted only one semester.

In 1875, when he was 19, Tesla traveled to Graz, Austria, to begin his college education. He attended the Polytechnic School, which was considered one of the best schools in the empire for science and engineering. Tesla, as he had as a boy, pushed himself to succeed. He later wrote:

Electricity wasn't the only lifelong interest that Nikola Tesla explored in college. Sparked by his desire to fly, Tesla described to one teacher an idea for a "flying machine … one based on sound, scientific principles." This was about 25 years before the American inventors Orville and Wilbur Wright tested the first successful engine-powered airplane. Tesla claimed in 1919 that his early flying machine would soon be ready for use, but he never produced an actual aircraft. He did, however, sketch ideas for several aircraft.

[D]uring the whole first year I regularly started my work at three o'clock in the morning and continued until eleven at night, no Sundays or holidays excepted. As most of my fellow-students took things easily, naturally enough I eclipsed [passed] all records.

Some of his professors worried that Tesla would kill himself with so little sleep and so much hard work.

In college Tesla studied math, several kinds of science, including physics and chemistry, and several foreign languages. He had great skill with languages and would eventually speak French, English, German, and Italian, along with Serbian and related languages. On his own he read the works of great writers from around the world.

Tesla also founded a club for Serbian students at the college. The members discussed serious subjects but also took time for fun. Tesla, who had a good sense of humor, gave one light-hearted talk called "About Noses." The club lasted for several decades after Tesla left the school.

In January 1877, during his second year at college, Tesla took a physics class that set him on the path to his greatest discovery. The professor brought in a new machine called the Gramme dynamo. The device had

The Gramme dynamo used wheels and belts to generate electricity.

a crank that when turned would generate electricity. If electricity from another source were fed into the machine, it could work as a motor.

The Gramme dynamo worked with direct current (DC) electricity. Sitting in class, Tesla thought it would be easier if the machine ran without its special brushes, since this would reduce the sparking that occurred with the DC operation. Tesla expressed his ideas to the professor, who quickly responded, "Mr. Tesla may accomplish great things, but he certainly never will do this."

Tesla could not accept the professor's certainty about DC electricity and the motor. DC electricity was simple to create with a battery. Static electricity and lightning also created DC power, but Tesla knew that powering a DC motor was not easy. While electricity flows in one direction, the electrons that make up electricity don't naturally move the same way. They rapidly change their direction, or alternate, as they move along. Special parts, called commutators and brushes, were needed with DC motors and generators to force the electrons to move in just one direction. For several years Tesla visualized various motors and generators. He couldn't find the key to solving the problem of creating an effective AC generator and motor, but he was not ready to give up.

During this time Tesla began to run out of money to pay for school. He asked a Serbian organization for help, but it refused. Tesla began gambling, and though at times he won, more often he lost. His father became angry when he learned about the losses. His mother came to Tesla with a roll of cash and told him, "Go and enjoy yourself. The sooner you lose all we possess, the better it will be." Tesla realized then that he had a gambling problem that could ruin his family, so he decided to quit. He also quit school, leaving without a degree.

The Reverend Milutin Tesla (1819–1879)

Tesla headed next to the Austro-Hungarian province of Slovenia, which bordered Austrian Croatia, to look for work. At the urging of his father, he returned home to Gospic. He was home when his father died in 1879. The Reverend Tesla had asked his son to finish his schooling in Prague, the capital of what is now the Czech Republic. Now Tesla wanted to carry out his father's wish.

Tesla entered the University of Prague. He continued his studies in math and science and still thought about building an AC motor. But after just one term,

In Tesla's boyhood, the telegraph was the most advanced form of long-distance communication. Electric current flowed along wires strung across poles. By quickly turning the current on and off in set patterns, an operator could send messages in a special code. The code was named for the American inventor who had perfected the telegraph, Samuel F.B. Morse. By the time Tesla was in college, the telephone had been invented. As a person speaks into it, the energy waves created by sound turn into an electrical current that also can be sent along wires. At the other end, the electrical signal is turned back into sound waves for the listener to hear.

he decided to leave school and look for work in Budapest, the capital of Hungary. A new phone system was being installed, and Tesla had heard that men with a background in electrical engineering could get jobs.

Arriving in Budapest in 1881, Tesla learned that the new phone system was not running yet. He took a job with the government in its main telegraph office. When the phone company finally opened, Tesla did a variety of jobs, including repairing equipment. He also learned about induction—transferring electricity or magnetism between two objects without their coming into contact. Induction would soon play a part in Tesla's first great scientific discovery.

The young engineer was still trying to perfect an AC motor. A health problem, however, almost ended that effort—and his life. Tesla suffered what he called a nervous breakdown. His body experienced powerful, odd sensations. He described his experience years later: "The sun rays ... would cause

Budapest, near the turn of the 20th century

blows of such force on my brain that they would stun me." He said that when he passed under a bridge, "I experienced a crushing pressure on my skull. … My pulse varied from a few to two hundred and sixty beats." A doctor was convinced Tesla would die. Tesla later wrote that his "powerful desire to live and to continue the work" helped keep him alive.

A little later, while still recovering from his illness, Tesla and a friend took a walk in a city park. Tesla was reciting some of his favorite poetry by a German poet. As he later recalled, "As I uttered these inspiring words the idea came like a flash of lightning and in an instant the truth was revealed. … I cannot begin to describe my emotions." With a stick in the sand, Tesla drew a picture of his AC motor.

Tesla, like all electrical engineers, knew that

> *All magnets have a north and south pole, and their pull is strongest at those poles. One magnet's north pole attracts another's south, while two like poles push away from each other. In a motor, electric current causes the poles on one set of magnets to constantly switch from north to south and back again. This set of magnets is often on a nonmoving part called a stator. The switching of the polarity of the magnets on the stator constantly attracts other magnets attached to a moving part in the motor called the rotor. The constantly switching poles and the continuing attraction make the rotor spin. The spinning rotor provides the power to run whatever is connected to the motor.*

magnetism and electricity have a special relationship. Passing a fixed magnet in and out of a coiled metal wire creates electricity. The magnet stirs electrons in the wire, even though it never touches the wire—a form of induction. Electricity sent through a coiled metal wire can turn it into a type of magnet called an electromagnet. One coiled wire is called a circuit. Using electricity, fixed magnets, and electromagnets together, scientists created the first simple electric motor.

Tesla used magnetism and induction to create an AC motor. AC current sent into the magnets in the stator switched their polarity automatically, ending the need for the commutator and brushes used on DC motors. This set up a rotating magnetic field in the stator's magnets that, through induction, caused the rotator to spin. The different sets of magnets had to be arranged at a certain angle to each other for this to work. Tesla also used two separate currents, so one was always strong

Tesla spent years perfecting his induction motors.

enough to keep the magnetic field moving.

For several months Tesla thought out all the details of his motor. It would take several more years for him to build one. He may or may not have known that other scientists had done work with rotating magnetic fields. In the years to come, however, he would be the first to perfect AC motors and power generation using these rotating fields. To do that, though, he needed money and the help of other skilled people. ᖶ

4 HEADING TO AMERICA

❧❧❧

At the Budapest telephone company, Nikola Tesla had impressed his boss with his skills. Shortly after Tesla first visualized his AC motor, the boss asked whether he wanted to start a new job. Thomas Edison was setting up companies in Europe to provide electric power for lighting and streetcars. The boss's brother worked at the Edison company in Paris, France, and needed help. Tesla jumped at the chance to work for the famous Edison and learn more about electricity.

Tesla soon began working at the Edison Continental Company. He learned how to set up the generating stations that created power for Edison's lamps. To his co-workers, Tesla sometimes talked about his motor. They seemed more impressed with his skill at billiards, a game he had learned to play

Thomas Edison held more than 1,000 patents. His dynamo generated power for the first electrical lighting system in New York.

during his college years. Tesla's new bosses, however, appreciated his great knowledge of electricity as he created a better way to make DC generators.

Tesla and the other engineers at the company traveled across France and Germany, setting up power stations. Starting in early 1883, Tesla spent almost a year in Strasbourg, which was then part of Germany but is now in eastern France. In his free time, he built a working model of his induction motor. When Tesla returned to Paris, he hoped the Edison company would reward him for all his efforts and for his earlier work with the generators. He asked several managers for a raise, and each said the others could do that. But none of them did. Tesla realized that he would never get the money he knew he deserved.

Early in 1884, Tesla got something even better than a raise—the chance to work for Thomas Edison himself. Edison's top assistant, Charles Batchelor, ran the Paris operations. He knew about Tesla's talents with electricity, and he arranged a job for Tesla in New York. The Serbian inventor had tried to talk to Edison's employees in Paris about his motor, but no one seemed interested. Edison created DC power with his generators. Perhaps in America, Tesla could show what he knew to be true—AC power was easier to use than DC. If he could not convince Edison, maybe he could find money to create his own AC system.

Before Tesla left Paris, two of his uncles gave him money to help pay for the trip. Unfortunately some of his money and belongings were stolen before he reached the train station. Tesla still managed to reach the port, where he boarded a steamship for the voyage across the Atlantic Ocean.

Tesla arrived in New York in 1884 and would call the city home until his death in 1943.

Tesla landed in a bustling New York City and soon had a chance to show his skills. Walking by a small machine shop, he saw the owner struggling to repair an electric machine. Tesla later reported, "I took off my coat and went to work, [and] … had it running perfectly in an hour."

Tesla soon met Edison for the first time. Edison had won worldwide fame for his work with lighting

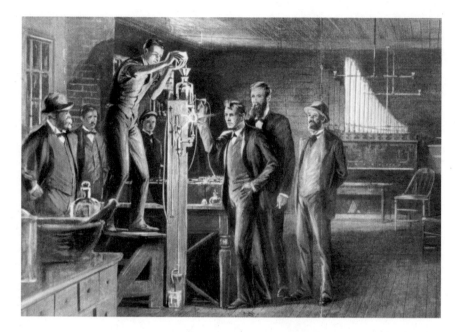

Edison (center) and an assistant worked on an incandescent lightbulb.

and for creating the phonograph, which recorded and played back sound. Now Edison was trying to light up the United States with his DC power stations, connected to his bulbs. "The meeting with Edison," Tesla wrote in *My Inventions*, "was a memorable event in my life." The two men could not look less alike. Tesla, at more than 6 feet (180 centimeters) tall, towered over the much shorter Edison. Tesla always wore fine clothes and appeared neat and clean, while Edison often looked like a slob.

Unlike Tesla, Edison had barely gone to school. Tesla was amazed that a man with almost no formal education could invent so brilliantly. Years later, however, Tesla had a different view of Edison and his approach to inventing. Tesla said Edison's method "was inefficient in the extreme … just a little theory and calculation would have saved him 90 percent of the labor [effort]."

Still an unknown inventor himself, Tesla was glad to be working for such a famous man. Tesla had a chance to impress Edison just a few weeks after he arrived in New York. The S.S. *Oregon*, one of the fastest ships of the day, was sitting in the harbor. Its lighting system, which had been designed by Edison, was not working. Tesla took his tools down to the ship and worked through the night. With some help from the crew, he repaired the generator and had the lights on again. Around 5 in the morning, Tesla finally headed back to Edison's shop. Coming out of the building were Edison, Batchelor, and several other men. Edison joked that Tesla was running around all night having fun. No, Tesla told him, he had fixed the generators on the *Oregon*. Tesla later described Edison's reaction: "He looked at me in silence and walked away without another word. But when he had gone some distance I

Thomas Edison (1847–1931) is considered one of the world's greatest inventors. Like Tesla he was familiar with telegraph systems. Some of Edison's first inventions improved how messages were sent. He also improved the first telephone before perfecting his incandescent bulb and inventing the phonograph. In the years that followed, Edison also helped create some of the first motion picture cameras and projectors.

Edison's electrical power station was featured in Scientific American *in 1891.*

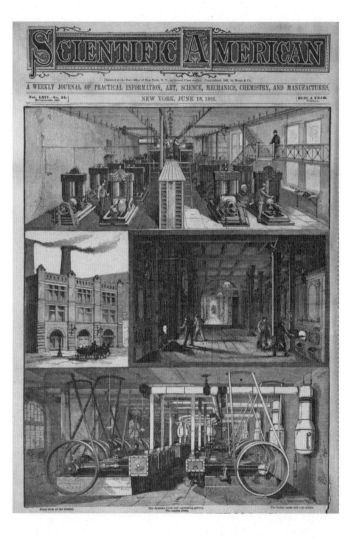

heard him remark, 'Batchelor, this is a good man.'"

Tesla normally started his workday at 10:30 in the morning and worked until 5 the next morning. His hard work impressed Edison, and he liked Tesla's ideas for improving the DC generators used to create electricity in his power stations. He told Tesla,

"There's fifty thousand dollars in it for you—if you can do it." With Tesla then earning just $18 per week, that amount was a fortune. He eagerly began the new job, which lasted for months.

Tesla also had something else on his mind. He later wrote: "All this time I was getting more and more anxious about the invention [AC motor] and was making up my mind to place it before Edison." At one point, while meeting Edison at Coney Island, an amusement park, Tesla finally found the courage to bring up his AC motor. Just at that instant, a man came up to Edison and attracted his attention. Tesla remained silent about his invention.

Nikola Tesla at age 29

When he finished his work on the generators, Tesla went to Edison to collect his bonus. The offer of the $50,000, Tesla learned, was just a joke. Edison would not pay him anything extra for his hard work. Not liking Edison's sense of humor, Tesla quit the company.

A lawyer Tesla had met while working for Edison soon helped Tesla get his first U.S. patents. He had made improvements to generators and to arc lamps, electric lights used outdoors. Through the lawyer, Tesla met two men willing to help him start his own company. By 1886, the Tesla Electric Light and Manufacturing Company was open for business. Ads for the company promised that Tesla's arc lamps provided "absolute safety and a great saving of power."

Tesla's partners, however, were not interested in his AC motor. In the end, they did not care much about Tesla either. Once the company was up and running, they forced out the inventor and took control for themselves. As winter approached, Tesla found himself with no job and no money. "There were

Tesla's alternating current generator

many days," he later wrote, "when [I] did not know where my next meal was coming from." To survive, he took a job digging ditches. He often fought severe headaches—perhaps the pain of knowing his talents were being ignored.

Luck, though, was on Tesla's side. His boss on the digging crew learned about his talents as an engineer, and the boss happened to know Alfred S. Brown. Like Tesla, Brown was an engineer, and he had worked with arc lamps. Also, like the Serbian inventor, Brown thought AC offered a better source of electric power than DC.

With Brown's help, Tesla found new investors who would back him. The Tesla Electric Company soon began making AC induction motors in New York City, and the company filed its first patent in April 1887. Tesla refined his original motors, adding more circuits, and then designed his own AC generator.

Other inventors had already created AC generators. Tesla had used one when he built the first models of his motor. In the United States, some power companies were already providing electricity to lights using AC power. Tesla, however, was about to tell the world about his new system, which was unlike anything else that existed. ✑

5 SUCCESS AND MORE RESEARCH

&c&x&o

In the United States, George Westinghouse had been the first person to provide AC power to customers. Like Thomas Edison, he was both an inventor and a businessman. Westinghouse often bought patents held by other investors. In 1885, he read about a new device that would change the delivery of electric power.

Westinghouse realized that AC power could be sent over long distances at high voltage. An increase in voltage means more current is flowing through the wires. He knew, though, that the voltage needed to send the AC over long distances was too powerful for an electric light. To power a light, the voltage had to be transformed, or brought to a lower level. When Westinghouse read about such a transformer, he saw a way to compete with Edison and his power company.

Tesla's alternating current power system lit the many white lights of the 1893 Columbian Exhibition, which was called the White City.

George Westinghouse's first inventions were for railroads. One helped put cars back on the track after they accidentally came off. His most famous was the air brake, which could stop all the cars of a moving train at once. Westinghouse (1846–1914) set up a company to make the brakes, then began buying patents for electrical signals used along railroad tracks. From there, Westinghouse moved into electric lighting, first using a DC system and then an AC system. He later entered the radio business and made stoves, refrigerators, and other appliances.

DC power could travel only a short distance over electrical wires and into homes. This meant Edison had to build many small power stations close to his customers. AC power and a transformer, Westinghouse saw, provided a different way to deliver power. The generating station could be hundreds of miles away from the customers. The power would travel at high voltage over long distances, then be "stepped down," or lowered, close to the customers. One station could serve many more customers than Edison's small DC stations.

Westinghouse began to buy patents so he could create an AC power system for lights. By the end of 1886, incandescent bulbs running on AC power provided by Westinghouse were glowing in Massachusetts and New York. Another company also competed to deliver AC power. The current in these new systems traveled farther than Edison's DC current, but not by much. The distances Westinghouse imagined were still not possible with the system he used. But in New York, Nikola Tesla had the answer to Westinghouse's dreams.

By early 1888 Tesla had built several AC motors, generators, and transformers. His transformers could either step down or step up (increase) the voltage as needed. The inventor filed for even more patents, and he drew the attention of T.C. Martin, a journalist who specialized in electricity. Martin realized that Tesla was doing something new and great, and he asked William Anthony, a professor of electrical engineering, to look over the induction motor. The professor, too, was impressed. They persuaded Tesla to tell the world about his inventions.

In May 1888, Tesla gave a lecture in Philadelphia to other scientists and engineers, describing

Tesla held nearly 300 patents.

his work with AC power. He noted that his health was not the best—perhaps a result of all his hard work of the previous months. Then he described his work with rotating magnetic fields and his ability to get rid of brushes and commutators in his motor.

He described the entire process for generating AC power, sending it over long distances, and using it to power his motor. His inventions, Tesla said, "will at once establish the superior adaptability of these [AC] currents to the transmission of power and will show … results which are very much desired in the practical operation of such systems and which cannot be accomplished by means of continuous [DC] currents."

Professor Anthony then spoke about Tesla's motor, noting it needed less power than DC motors and had fewer moving parts. Another professor in the audience, Elihu Thomson, then rose and said he had already been working on his own AC induction motor. Tesla politely informed Thomson that his motor was not quite the same, since it still relied

Tesla's two-phase motor was featured in an 1893 Westinghouse exhibit.

on brushes. Tesla knew he had created something completely different.

In the following months George Westinghouse went to work. He was convinced that Tesla's patents would give him a new and better way to create and send AC power. He made Tesla an offer—$60,000 in cash and shares in Westinghouse's company, plus royalties on the power sold to customers.

Tesla accepted the offer and spent parts of 1888 and 1889 in Pittsburgh, Pennsylvania, the home of the Westinghouse Electric Company. For several years the company tried to make Tesla's motor work with its AC system. Finally the engineers accepted Tesla's system. His motor worked best with 60 switches of the current's direction per second—called cycles—making it more conve-nient than the 133 cycles Westinghouse had used in the past.

George Westinghouse (1846–1914)

As this work went on, Tesla and Westinghouse gained a powerful enemy—Tesla's old boss, Thomas

Edison. Since the first AC power systems had appeared, Edison had tried to convince people they were unsafe. He did not want Westinghouse and other AC companies to take away business from his DC system. When Westinghouse teamed up with Tesla, Edison increased his attacks on AC power. The battle between Edison and Westinghouse over AC and DC was later called the Battle of the Currents.

Edison let an electrical engineer named H.P. Brown come to his labs and give powerful electric shocks to small animals. Brown used AC power to electrocute them. People could die from shocks from DC power, but Brown and Edison wanted to show the world that AC was much more deadly. Lower voltages of AC killed animals, while the same voltage of DC only startled and hurt them a bit.

Brown did some of his work using Westinghouse motors, and the press reported on his results. *The New York Times* said Brown's work showed "the alternating current to be the most deadly force known to science." Soon the word used to describe such electrocutions was "Westinghousings." Westinghouse wrote to newspapers, defending the overall safety of AC power and pointing out DC was not entirely harmless. Edison countered by saying AC power should be illegal.

Late in 1888, Edison and Brown scored a major victory when New York officials decided to use alternating current to kill convicted murderers. In 1890, the state carried out the first execution by electrocution. The death was not quick, as state officials had hoped, since the amount of voltage sent into the man's body was too low. Even Edison was somewhat sickened by the reports of the slow, gruesome death. Westinghouse said, "They could have done better with an axe." Tesla hated the idea that AC power was being used this way. Years later he wrote that with execution by alternating current, people "are not dispatched [killed] in a merciful manner but literally roasted alive."

In their battle with Edison, however, Tesla and Westinghouse had demand on their side. More cities were buying power for lights from Westinghouse. AC was also being used to power streetcars. The ability

Convicted murderer William Kemmler was the first person to die in the electric chair.

to send AC over long distances was the most important feature. With careful use, AC was safe. As AC systems became popular, some companies began to copy Tesla's work, and Westinghouse had to sue them to protect his control of Tesla's patents.

To better compete with Westinghouse, in 1892 Edison's electric company merged with another, creating General Electric. Edison had no control of the new company, which began to explore ways to create its own AC system. But there was one major problem: Tesla's work was the key to creating any workable AC system, and Westinghouse held the patents for the United States. (In Europe a system based on Tesla's work had already sent AC electricity long distances. Soon Westinghouse would do the same.)

The value of AC power went on display in 1893, when Westinghouse won the right to power the lights at the 1893 World's Columbian Exhibition in Chicago, Illinois. This fair was in honor of Christopher Columbus' voyage to North America in 1492. Relying on AC equipment based on Tesla's designs, Westinghouse used 10 huge genera-

General Electric began as a company that made power equipment and incandescent lightbulbs. Since Tesla's time the company has expanded into many other areas, including making airplane engines, home appliances, and wind turbines. General Electric also makes systems for generating electricity. In addition, the company owns NBC Universal, a national television company and movie studio. Like Westinghouse, it still sells lightbulbs.

The World's Columbian Exhibition featured the first Ferris wheel. The giant ride's 36 wooden cars could each hold 60 people.

tors to power about 170,000 electric lights. Exhibits throughout the fairgrounds also had AC power for motors. At a time when electricity was still rare in homes, millions of Americans got to see electricity at work as they never had before.

The fairgoers also saw Tesla. Westinghouse gave him space to display information about his inventions. The exhibit included a small working model of his AC generation and transmission system. Tesla dazzled the crowd with the great sparks he created as electricity passed through him, the result of his projects during the years leading up to the fair. ✍

6

FROM ELECTRICITY TO RADIO

During the years of the Battle of the Currents and up to the Columbian Exhibition, Nikola Tesla had continued to work hard in his lab. He still slept only a few hours a night, though he took time to dine regularly at New York City's finest restaurants. Tesla became friendly with well-known people and loved to attend their dinners. With so much of his time devoted to work, he never married or had a family of his own. Through letters, though, he kept in touch with relatives in Austrian Croatia, often sending them money. They, in turn, wrote him often, thanking him for his generosity.

Moving from his work with induction motors, Tesla began to explore high-frequency alternating current. By the 1880s, scientists had known that light

An 1890s magazine article, titled "The New Wizard of the West," featured an illustration of Tesla holding balls of flame.

was one form of electromagnetic energy. This energy is also called radiation, and other forms include microwaves, which can cook food, and radio waves. The various forms of electromagnetic energy travel in the shape of waves. Each wave has a high point and a low point. Wavelength is the distance from the high point of one wave to the high point of the next. One complete wave is called an oscillation. The wavelength of visible light is tiny, while some radio waves can be miles long.

Electromagnetic waves also have various frequencies, which measure how many complete waves pass by a point in one second. Tesla began working on a machine that would create electricity with extremely high frequencies and voltages. High-frequency AC, he knew, would be less dangerous to humans because it safely passed through the body. It also could be transmitted more easily. Tesla created oscillators, machines that could generate various high-frequency currents. The frequencies created by his oscillators were so precise that they could be used to keep time, and Tesla used one to run a clock. His oscillators were also known as Tesla coils, and other engineers began using them to create high-frequency energy.

Working with high-frequency electricity, Tesla discovered that it could travel through the air. He designed a new kind of lightbulb made from a sealed glass with gases inside. The tube glowed from the airborne electricity. This bulb and another kind, later called the fluorescent bulb, did not have the tiny wire filaments that glow inside incandescent bulbs. Tesla also lit up glass tubes filled with gas, creating the colorful neon light. These lights are used today for advertising and as art.

Rumors spread about the new work Tesla was doing in his New York lab. In 1891, he finally began speaking publicly about his latest discoveries and

To demonstrate "wireless energy," Tesla held a gas-filled tube operated by a high-frequency oscillator.

Oscillators, also called Tesla coils, created high-frequency, high-voltage electricity.

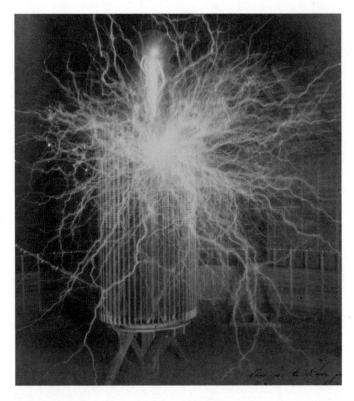

inventions. In New York he spent three hours on a stage, amazing other scientists and engineers. He showed machines that created bursts of electrostatic energy—static electricity—that formed various shapes. He demonstrated his new bulbs, including one he held in his hand as he touched one of his oscillators. Special shoes with cork soles insulated him, protecting him from electric shock. The audience sat in wonder as the voltage passed through Tesla's body and made the bulb in his hand glow. At the end of his talk, Tesla said:

Among many observations, I have only selected those which I thought might interest you. The field is wide and completely unexplored ... all around us everything is spinning, everything is moving, everywhere is energy.

Tesla gave a similar talk in London the next year, to an audience that included some of the most famous British scientists of the day. A reporter wrote that Tesla left them "spellbound," while Tesla said his chief aim was to "advance ideas which I am hopeful will serve as starting points of new departures." Tesla had learned from and been inspired by many of the men in the room that night. He hoped his ideas would inspire them, too.

Tesla spent several months in Europe. He visited other scientists and then went to Austrian Croatia to visit his family. His mother was dying, and he stayed at her side until he was forced to rest. Lying in bed, he dreamed of an angelic figure who looked like his mother. Then, he later wrote, "I was awaked by an indescribably sweet song of many voices." The dream and voices, he thought, were signs his mother had died, and later he found out she had. For a time Tesla wondered whether some supernatural power was at work. But after many months of research, he decided that something he had seen before he went to bed—a painting of angels—had caused his dream.

And music from a nearby church had been the source of the singing voices he heard.

Returning to New York, Tesla began to research a new idea. Scientists had recently discovered radio waves, a form of high-frequency electromagnetism. Working with his oscillators, Tesla came to believe that high-frequency energy could be sent through the air from one point to another. The waves could be used to carry messages without any need for wires, as in telegraph and telephone systems. Tesla began building transmitters, which could create and then send out electrical signals through an antenna. He also made receivers, which would pick up a signal with its own antenna some distance away. Inside each device were circuits tuned to send or receive a certain frequency.

Tesla began testing his system in 1893, and in 1894 he told a reporter, "I look forward with absolute confidence to sending messages through

Tesla (left) watched as his good friend, author Mark Twain, participated in an experiment.

the earth without any wires." Some of his friends, however, thought his ideas were crazy, and they told him not to say too much about the "wireless," as radio was first called. They feared other scientists would not take him seriously anymore.

Through 1894 Tesla spent many afternoons on the roof of his lab, where he had set up a transmitter. Then he would go to various spots in New York with a receiver to see how far the radio signal could travel. On the receiving end, a string held onto a

Tesla's giant generators produced AC electricity at the Niagara Falls power plant.

balloon filled with hot gases that made it float high in the air. On top of the balloon was an antenna. By the end of 1894 Tesla was sending the signal a little over a mile. Soon he hoped he could make improvements to his equipment and send the signal up to 50 miles (80.5 km).

By this time Tesla's fame had spread. Work was complete on the hydroelectric power station at Niagara Falls, with Tesla's AC system at its core.

His AC system was providing electricity to cities around the country. Tesla was often written about in magazines. Sometimes he was compared to his old boss, Thomas Edison, as one of the great geniuses of electricity. Early in 1895, Tesla and some investors formed a new company that would make his generators, motors, and other devices. Then Tesla's good luck came to a sudden end.

Early on the morning of March 14, a fire broke out in Tesla's lab. When he came to work a few hours later, tears filled his eyes as he looked over the damage. The floor where he kept his equipment had collapsed and everything was burned. "It cannot be true," he said, pacing near the wreckage. He told *The New York Times:*

> *The work of half my lifetime, very nearly; all my mechanical instruments and scientific apparatus [equipment], that it has taken years to perfect, swept away in a fire that lasted only an hour or two.*

Although dazed, Tesla soon recovered. With money from investors he built a new lab and went back to work. There was still so much about the various forms of energy that he wanted to explore. ✍

7 ENERGY ALL AROUND

The late 1890s was an exciting time for scientists. Some of the best minds in the world were trying to understand electricity and other forms of electromagnetic energy. At the end of 1895 Wilhelm Conrad Röntgen of Germany announced the discovery of X-rays. This form of radiation passes through an object and creates an image of the object as its rays hit chemicals on a plate behind the object. Doctors soon learned that they could use X-rays to take pictures of bones inside the human body.

Tesla began experimenting with X-rays, which produced images that he called shadowgraphs. He took X-ray pictures of small animals, his assistants, and himself. At first Tesla thought the rays were relatively harmless, but he began to notice that they could

Tesla's huge steel and wooden tower at Wardenclyffe, Long Island, New York, was built to demonstrate wireless transmission of power.

burn the skin, and at times he suffered headaches while working with X-rays. He said that "in a severe case, the skin gets deeply colored and blackened in places, and ugly … blisters form." Tesla saw the need to have a protective shield when working with X-rays. Today patients in dentists' offices are draped with lead sheets when receiving some X-rays.

Tesla also did work on radio-controlled devices, which he called automatons, or robots. In 1898, he demonstrated a remote-controlled boat in a tank at Madison Square Garden in New York. The device moved in all directions, and Tesla could also turn on and off lights mounted on the tiny vessel. Tesla thought the government might use other versions of his robotic boat to attack enemy ships during war. He later recalled how a government official "burst out in laughter upon my telling him what I had accomplished." To some people Tesla's work seemed like something from a fairy tale, not real science. He constantly had to prove himself and his work.

Tesla also suggested that one day a car could be driven by remote control, and a person would not even have to see an automaton to control it. Today his vision is a reality. Using computers and video cameras, the U.S. military can control small planes without pilots and use them to track down and kill enemy troops. In addition, robotically controlled rovers have moved across the surface of Mars.

Through the late 1890s, and for the rest of his life, Tesla was fascinated with the idea of sending electricity great distances. Wanting more space and privacy, in May 1899 he left New York for Colorado Springs, Colorado. In a laboratory with a roof that opened to the sky, he built his largest Tesla coil ever. Attached to the oscillator was a 200-foot-tall (61 m) copper pole with a large copper ball on top. Tesla believed each layer of air above Earth was filled with a particular frequency of energy. Somehow, he believed, he could use those frequencies to transmit electric power. Tesla also thought that waves of electricity could be sent through Earth itself. Either way, the need for wires would end.

When he tested his device, he watched with pleasure as it created bolts of electric energy more than 100 feet (30.5 m) long. Then the machine went silent. Tesla had blown out equipment at the local electric company, the source of the AC power he used for his generator.

At one point during his Colorado work Tesla thought he had made a remarkable discovery—life on

During the 1930s, one of Tesla's oldest inventions played a featured part in a famous movie. The makers of the film Frankenstein *used a Tesla coil to create huge sparks of electricity. The coil was part of the equipment shown in the lab of Dr. Frankenstein, the scientist in the movie who creates a living monster from dead bodies. About 40 years later, the same Tesla coil was used again during the filming of* Young Frankenstein, *a comedy based on the original movie.*

A double-exposure publicity photo featured Tesla in his Colorado experimental station. With a huge roar, the largest Tesla coil ever built sent electrical discharges more than 20 feet (6 m).

other planets. He claimed to have received three short radio signals from outer space. Today some people think he really did detect radio signals from space. More likely, though, he picked up the signal being sent during a radio experiment on Earth. But whatever the explanation, Tesla wrote in 1900:

> That we can send a message to a planet is certain, that we can get an answer is probable: man is not the only being in the Infinite [universe] gifted with a mind.

Radio experiments going on while Tesla was in

Colorado were part of the work of a young Italian scientist. Since 1896, Guglielmo Marconi had been experimenting with radio. That year he sent a message in Morse code more than a mile using radio signals. In 1899, he sent messages over even greater distances.

Tesla knew about Marconi's work. He also knew that the Italian was using some of Tesla's oscillators to send radio signals. Tesla had filed for his first U.S. radio patent in 1897 and received it in 1900. When Marconi filed for his own patent that year, he was turned down. His work was not original, since it relied on Tesla's oscillator to work. But Marconi continued to develop a radio system, winning support from Thomas Edison and others.

Tesla, however, believed he could create a system that would send either electricity or radio signals around the globe. He imagined building a huge transmitter that could send out the signals. Tesla had been short of money for several

Some of Tesla's work in 1898 involved what he called a mechanical oscillator. The machine created frequencies that could cause objects to move. On one occasion, he attached the oscillator to an iron pipe in his room. The frequencies traveled through the pipe and into surrounding buildings. They began to shake as if an earthquake had hit New York City. Some people later called the device Tesla's earthquake machine, and he said whole buildings could be brought down if they were hit with the right frequency. Later he claimed he could split the world apart using explosives, if he timed them to the vibrations that naturally occur in Earth.

years. In 1897, he had agreed to give up the royalties George Westinghouse had promised him for the AC power system. Westinghouse had his own money problems at the time, and Tesla readily agreed to help his friend—the man who had believed in the worth of his invention. Now Tesla had to find a new source of money, and he turned to J.P. Morgan.

Tesla spent most of his adult life in New York, but he also worked in other cities in the United States.

Based in New York, Morgan was perhaps the most powerful banker in the world. He was about to create the world's largest company, U.S. Steel, and he controlled railroads and other large businesses. Morgan knew that some people considered Tesla odd. But he

also knew that Tesla's system had harnessed the power of Niagara Falls. Perhaps, Morgan thought, he could make money from the inventor's work. Morgan agreed to give Tesla $150,000. In return the inventor would give Morgan just over half of any money made from patents that came out of Tesla's new work.

Tesla poured out his thanks in a letter, calling the banker a "great generous man! My work will proclaim loudly your name to the world." He also promised Morgan that his investment would soon be worth millions.

With the money Tesla bought some land on Long Island and began to build. He called the site Wardenclyffe. The centerpiece was a tower almost 200 feet (61 m) tall, topped with a 68-foot-wide (20.7 m) dome. Under the tower was a shaft that plunged almost as deep into the ground.

As Tesla worked at the site, he and the rest of the world received shocking news. Marconi had sent the first radio message across the Atlantic. He would soon become famous as the "father" of the radio.

Tesla was not the only great scientist and inventor who did early work in radio. Germany's Heinrich Hertz was the first person to detect radio waves and study their speed. A Canadian, Reginald Fessenden, worked with radio waves to carry voices, as opposed to electric signals in Morse code, as Marconi did. Fessenden sent his first wireless message with a human voice in 1900. In the years that followed, Lee DeForest and Edwin Armstrong made advances that led to the creation of practical radios that were easy to use.

Tesla, lacking money, could not afford to sue Marconi for illegally using his patents. Besides, Tesla's own system of wireless transmission, he believed, would have a greater impact than Marconi's work.

Early in 1902, Tesla needed more money for his Wardenclyffe project. Morgan said no. Marconi had shown that long-distance wireless communication was possible—and could be done fairly cheaply. Morgan did not see the need to spend money on Tesla's more expensive idea. Further, Morgan was not interested in the wireless transmission of power. Some historians say Morgan did not want Tesla to succeed. Morgan and other investors controlled General Electric, which already provided electric power over wires. They did not want Tesla to create a system that might reduce the price of transmitting electricity, which would mean less money for GE. Other historians suggest Morgan lacked faith in Tesla's ability. Tesla had grand ideas and did marvelous things, but he rarely made money with his inventions. Tesla himself knew others saw him this way. "My enemies have been so successful in portraying me as a poet and visionary [dreamer], that I must put out something commercial without delay."

At times Tesla received money when manufacturers sold medical equipment using his coil. Certain frequencies of electricity seemed to help treat some physical problems, such as arthritis, a joint disease. Still, Tesla had debts and needed huge amounts of money to finish his work at Wardenclyffe. He continued to write Morgan, and later, Morgan's son, asking for help. At times he sounded angry. Other times he seemed to plead: "Are you going to leave me in a hole?!!" The Morgans never budged. Work stopped at Wardenclyffe, though Tesla never lost hope that someday he could send electricity long distances without wires.

8 More Grand Ideas

⚜

Through the early 1900s, Nikola Tesla lived as he always had since arriving in the United States. For many years he stayed at the Waldorf-Astoria, one of New York's finest hotels. He ate at fancy restaurants, and he always wore neat, stylish clothes. The tall, well-dressed inventor was a well-known figure on the streets of New York. By 1905 his money was tight and, as in the past, he sometimes battled illness. He wrote George Scherff, a trusted assistant, "Troubles and troubles, but they do just seem to track me."

Struggling through his troubles, Tesla began working on a new project—a new kind of turbine. Most turbines had blades, which turned as water or air streamed past them. Tesla came up with a blade-less turbine. It had discs stacked together, with just small spaces separating them. The discs were attached to a central shaft inside a sealed metal holder. When fluid went past the discs, they turned the shaft, which could be used to create electricity, just like the turbines in Tesla's AC system at Niagara Falls. The bladeless turbine was another great invention. Tesla could provide more power with a smaller engine than anything else that existed.

In 1909, Tesla started a company to make the turbines, but as he developed them and made models, Tesla found a problem. The metals he used to make the discs could not stand the extremely fast speeds at which the turbine turned. They would crack and bend. As with his work on the wireless transmission of electric power, Tesla looked for investors to help him perfect his turbines. The work went on for decades, but he never produced one that worked correctly. Bladeless turbines were not perfected until the 1980s.

Through the 1910s Tesla's work on radio was the subject of several court battles. Guglielmo Marconi, in 1904, had won a huge legal battle. The U.S. Patent Office, which awards patents, reversed an earlier decision and gave Marconi the basic patents for the process of sending and receiving radio signals. In the years that followed, Marconi's company sued people making radios based on ideas in its patents. In a case in Germany Tesla defended one of the men Marconi had sued. Tesla said the man had used Tesla's patents, not Marconi's, and that Tesla's patents were still the basic patents for radio—despite what the Patent Office said.

Finally, in 1915, Tesla sued Marconi himself. For too long, Marconi had received credit for the radio, when Tesla and other electrical engineers knew that Tesla's work had come first. Marconi had even shared science's greatest award, the Nobel Prize, for his work in radio. Tesla, meanwhile, saw his work ignored.

Filing his suit, Tesla told *The New York Times*, "My patents describe a new and original wireless system. ... Long after their grant to me, Marconi filed an application and secured a patent which covers exactly the same fundamental arrangements." Tesla

A young Guglielmo Marconi with his machine for "telegraphy without wires"

said that a French court had just ruled for him in a similar case, recognizing that his important work in radio had come first. The legal battle with Marconi in the United States would drag on for decades. In the meantime, Tesla went on with his work.

His latest inventions included a speedometer for cars and a new headlight for train engines, and he continued to work on his robotic, radio-controlled devices. In 1915, he also gave his first public description of what was later called the death ray. Tesla said the beam of electricity would travel at 300 miles (483 km) per second, and its "great destructive effects can be produced at any point on the globe … and with great accuracy." Tesla added, however, that the time was not right to talk about the details of this device. World War I was going on in Europe, and Tesla seemed to fear how it would be used. Or perhaps the ray was not as developed as he seemed to suggest. During the war

Tesla also proposed using rays of energy to detect submarines, which Germany was using to attack ships. This idea became a reality with the development of radar during the 1930s, though Tesla was not involved with it.

Through this period money remained hard for Tesla to find. He had to give up his land on Long Island to pay debts, and he constantly looked for new investors for his work. He also increasingly worked for other companies, offering his vast knowledge in return for money.

The image of Tesla as a world-famous figure was

Tesla gave the deed to Wardencluffe to the Waldorf-Astoria to cover more than $20,000 in hotel bills.

starting to fade. His work on AC power was becoming a distant memory to the American public. His project on Long Island was over, ending his best effort to send power and radio signals around the world. He never lost hope, though, that he would achieve that goal. He continued to work in his lab. Just a few years before, he had told an audience, "There is no enjoyment that I could picture in my mind so exquisite as the triumph which follows an original invention or discovery."

In 1917, Tesla received an honor that showed some people had not forgotten his talents and inventions. He won the Edison Medal. The American Institute of Electrical Engineers presented the award, which was named for Thomas Edison.

Tesla at age 64

Tesla had spoken to that group almost 30 years before, describing the induction motor that made him famous. At first he wanted to refuse the medal. He thought something named for Edison would bring more attention to the Wizard of Menlo Park than to Tesla himself, but finally he agreed to accept it. At a dinner in his honor,

Tesla even managed to say some nice things about his first boss in the United States. Tesla called Edison a "wonderful man." B.A. Behrend, vice president of the institute, had nice things to say about Tesla when he presented the award:

> *Were we to seize and to eliminate from our industrial world the results of Mr. Tesla's work, the wheels of industry would cease to turn, our electric cars and trains would stop, our towns would be dark, our mills would be dead and idle.*

Tesla's work with bladeless turbines went on, and he was still convinced he could perfect the concept and make millions of dollars. His legal battles continued, too, as Tesla tried to win money from people he thought were illegally using his patents. He won some of the cases but lost others. Tesla began to spend more time away from New York as he tried to develop his inventions with various companies.

Starting in 1919, Tesla began to write a series of magazine articles that described some of the events of his life. Those writings were later published as *My Inventions*. Tesla did not describe all of his work. He focused on the AC motor and power generation, radio, and robotic vessels. He also offered details of his early life and his thoughts on the human race and life on Earth. "There is in fact but one race, of many

Tesla's My Inventions *first appeared in* Electrical Experimenter *in 1919.*

Beginning: "My Inventions," by Nikola Tesla

FEB. 1919 20 CTS. **ELECTRICAL** OVER 175 ILLUST.
EXPERIMENTER
SCIENCE AND INVENTION

THE TESLA WIRELESS LIGHT
SEE PAGE 692

LARGEST CIRCULATION OF ANY ELECTRICAL PUBLICATION

colors," he wrote, and though people seemed to be independent of each other, "we are connected by invisible links." Tesla hoped people would find a way to see what they had in common instead of arguing over their differences. He hoped the world could avoid another world war, such as the one that had just ended in November 1918. His work on "death rays," he hoped, would help reach that goal. They would be used only for defense, to shoot down invading planes. He believed that because they feared the power of the rays, countries would not launch attacks on each other.

Tesla's peaceful, helpful nature also was evident in his daily life. For years, on his walks around New York, he fed the pigeons that fluttered around the streets and landed on the sidewalks. At times he took injured or sickly pigeons back to his hotel room and tried to nurse them back to health. A visitor to the room described seeing several dozen pigeons: "Some had wing diseases, others broken legs."

Tesla also created a special mixture of seeds and other foods for the birds, which he hoped to sell. That plan never worked out, but Tesla continued to enjoy the special relationship he had with birds. One in particular, he said, was his favorite: "I had only to wish and call her and she would come flying to me." As he neared his 70s Tesla spent more time with the birds. Many of his old friends had died, but Tesla did not slow down, continuing to travel to Chicago, Milwaukee, and other cities where he had work. He continued to explore energy in all its forms. ✎

TIME

The Weekly Newsmagazine

Keystone

NIKOLA TESLA*

All the world's his power house.

(See SCIENCE)

*From a portrait by Princess Lwoff-Parlaghy.

Chapter
9   FINAL YEARS

❦

In 1931, as Nikola Tesla turned 75, his friend, writer Kenneth Swezey, arranged a birthday celebration for him. Scientists from around the world sent letters praising Tesla for his work. Some wrote that Tesla's achievements and ideas had sparked their own research in electricity and radio. One of the letters came from Albert Einstein, considered then—and now—one of the world's greatest scientists. Einstein wrote: "I congratulate you on the magnificent success of your life's work." Tesla, however, disagreed with some of Einstein's ideas. A few years earlier, he had written a poem about scientists and called Einstein "a long haired crank." Tesla thought the old ideas in physics that Einstein challenged were still true.

Tesla's birthday also led *Time* magazine to feature

When he turned 75, a two-page article in Time *magazine celebrated Tesla's achievements.*

him on the cover and write a long article about him. The magazine said he was "pale but healthy, thin to ghostliness but strong and alert as ever." Tesla talked about a new form of energy he had discovered and said he would provide more details in the years to come. In his later years, Tesla often made such announcements to reporters about wonderful new discoveries, but he rarely followed through with more information.

Tesla also talked again about life on other planets:

> *I think that nothing can be more important than interplanetary [between planets] communication. It will certainly come some day. And the certitude that there are other human beings in the universe, working, suffering, struggling, like ourselves, will produce a magic effect on mankind and will form the foundation of a universal brotherhood that will last as long as humanity itself.*

While those kinds of ideas struck some people as odd, Tesla also continued to focus on more practical concerns. He had long been concerned about the wasting of natural resources, and he knew the supplies of coal, petroleum, and natural gas were limited. These resources are commonly used to create electrical power. Tesla wanted to find new sources of power. In 1931, he wrote an article about producing power from the oceans. He said the difference in temperature in the layers of seawater could be used to heat and cool fluids and produce steam. The steam could then power turbines. Tesla thought it would cost too much to create such a system, though today there are some in use, producing small amounts of power. Tesla also talked about generating power from the heat deep below Earth's surface, another method used at times today.

Through the 1930s, Tesla talked more about his idea for a new weapon based on energy. Newspapers again called it a death ray, but Tesla insisted it was not a ray, but huge amounts of energy particles. As a weapon designed to prevent an enemy attack, it would end war, Tesla thought.

That idea appeared in a 1937 article in which Tesla expressed his views on what the world would be like in the 21st century. He predicted that people would see the dangers of pollution and dirty water and find ways to clean Earth. He thought dangerous products such as

Long fascinated by the idea of flying, Tesla in 1928 received a patent—his last one—for an aircraft unlike any other at the time. The aircraft, with a spinning propeller on its top, first rose straight off the ground, like a helicopter. The propeller then moved down 90 degrees to the front of the aircraft, to move it forward. Tesla said his "flying flivver" could land on the roof of a building and would only cost $1,000. The inventor never built a working model of his plane, but similar aircraft exist today. They are known as Vertical Takeoff and Land planes.

An artist's concept of Tesla's belief that future wars would be a "mere contest" between machines appeared in a 1922 edition of Science and Invention.

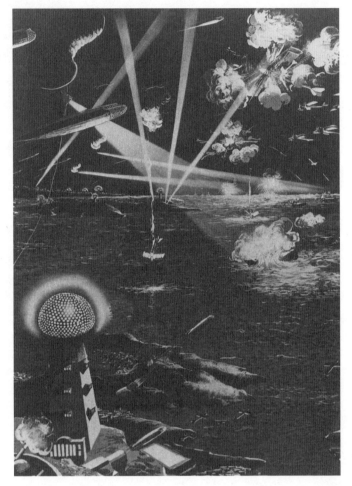

tobacco would become unpopular. He said, "It will simply be no longer fashionable to poison the system with harmful ingredients." Tesla also believed that before the 21st century, scientists would find a way to end droughts, forest fires, and floods. He probably would be disappointed to learn that this prediction did not come true.

Although Tesla hoped wars would one day end, he thought in 1937 that the world would first go through several more terrible military conflicts. That idea was not surprising—Japan, Germany, and Italy had already attacked other nations or threatened their neighbors. Two years later World War II began with Germany's invasion of Poland. By this time, Tesla had already written to the heads of several countries, including the United States, describing his new weapon. It came to be called a charged particle beam. The Soviet Union, which was made up of Russia and 14 other nations that are independent today, did some research on the charged particle beam. Years later, so did the United States. The weapon, however, has never been perfected.

Tesla hoped technology would bring an end to war.

By the time Tesla offered his idea of a new weapon, he was in his early 80s. As in the past, he sometimes had trouble paying bills, and his health had suffered greatly after an accident in 1937. While walking, he had been struck by a taxicab, breaking three of his ribs. Some aid came from the king and people of Yugoslavia. The nation then contained his old homeland of Austrian Croatia and the homeland of his ancestors, Serbia. Both the Yugoslav government and individual citizens began sending Tesla money every year. They wanted to show the world how proud they were of him and his deeds.

Tesla's name still appeared in newspapers when he talked about his particle beam weapon. In September 1940, the United States was aiding some of the nations fighting World War II, and the country was strengthening its own defenses. Tesla told *The New York Times* that his invention could melt the engines of enemy planes from 250 miles (402.5 km) away. The reporter wrote, "If Mr. Tesla really fulfills his promise the result achieved would be truly staggering."

When Germany invaded Yugoslavia, Tesla closely watched events in his homeland. He had been a proud U.S. citizen for many years, but he was sad for the Serbs, Croats, and other people of Yugoslavia. They had lost their freedom under German control. In 1942, Tesla met King Peter of Yugoslavia when he visited the United States. The aged inventor told him he hoped to live until Yugoslavia had regained its freedom.

Tesla, however, did not get his wish. While the war raged in Europe and Asia, Tesla died on January 7, 1943. More than 2,000 people attended a state funeral to honor him, and President Franklin Roosevelt and

his wife, Eleanor, praised Tesla for his work and service to the United States.

That service continued after the great inventor's death. Within days of his death, U.S. government officials reviewed all of his papers. They wanted to know exactly what research Tesla had done on his particle beam weapon and whether it could be useful for the military. A government scientist soon said there was nothing of value. Yet in the years that followed, government scientists continued to study copies of those papers. The original Tesla papers and other memorabilia are stored in the Nikola Tesla Museum in Belgrade, Serbia.

Later in the year he died, Tesla won his last great legal victory. The U.S. Supreme Court, the most powerful court in the country, ruled that Tesla, not Guglielmo Marconi, was the true inventor of radio. The court's decision also pointed out the important work done by other inventors before Marconi had applied for his patent. The decision ended the legal debate about the inventor of radio, but many books still give the credit to Marconi.

Tesla also did not receive full credit for his work with AC electricity. Some authors of early books on the subject ignored his work, either because they wanted credit or they supported other scientists who took credit. Later books continued to leave out Tesla's role. During the 1950s Tesla received attention, but not for his work in electricity. Some people who believed in unidentified flying objects (UFOs) and life on other planets began talking about Tesla. They claimed he had come from Venus to Earth to bring humans electricity and radio. These bizarre ideas did not help Tesla get the attention he deserved as a serious scientist and inventor. Since then, though, historians have helped restore Tesla's place as a unique and valuable thinker.

Some of his theories were wrong, scientists now know, but his ideas are still discussed. Some of the

A statue of Nikola Tesla was unveiled on the Canadian side of Niagara Falls in 2006. There is also a statue honoring Tesla on the American side.

inventions that he suggested were developed years later by others. What Tesla said about one of his ideas applies to many of them: "The world was not prepared for it. It was too far ahead of time." Plenty of his inventions, though, came just at the right time. Tesla and his work, especially on electricity and wireless communication, helped create the modern world. ᏋᎭ

TESLA'S LIFE

1856

Born July 10 in
Smiljan, Austrian
Croatia

1863

Tesla family
moves to Gospic

1873

Graduates from high
school in Karlovac

1865

1859

English scientist Charles
Darwin presents his theory
of evolution in his book,
The Origin of Species

1863

Construction begins
on the first trans-
continental railroad
in Sacramento,
California

1869

The periodic table of the
elements is invented by
Dimitri Mendeleev

WORLD EVENTS

1880

Studies for a time in Prague; takes a job in Budapest the following year

1882

Invents the rotating magnetic field and begins working for the Edison Continental Company in Paris

1875

Enters college in Graz, Austria

1880

1876

Alexander Graham Bell makes the first successful telephone transmission

1879

Thomas Edison perfects the incandescent lightbulb

1881

Booker T. Washington founds Tuskegee Institute

TESLA'S LIFE

1884

Comes to the
United States
and works for
Thomas Edison

1887

Begins making
his first induction
motors; sells the
patents on his AC
motors and power
generation to George
Westinghouse the
following year

1893

Sends wireless
transmission by
radio; Westinghouse
installs Tesla's AC
power system at the
World's Columbian
Exhibition in Chicago

1885

1884

The first practical
fountain pen is
invented by Lewis
Edson Waterman, a
45-year-old American
insurance broker

1886

Grover Cleveland
dedicates the Statue
of Liberty in New York
Harbor, a gift from the
people of France

1893

Financial crisis, the
Panic of 1893, hits
the United States;
unemployment
reaches 18 percent

WORLD EVENTS

1896

Sees operation of his AC system at Niagara Falls, the first AC hydroelectric power plant; experiments with X-rays

1899

Conducts experiments in Colorado Springs on wireless transmission of electricity

1901

Begins construction of transmitter at Wardenclyffe on Long Island, New York

1900

1896

The first modern Olympic Games are held in Athens, Greece

1898

The Spanish-American War gains Cuba its independence; Spain cedes the Philippines, Guam, and Puerto Rico to the United States for $20 million

1903

Brothers Orville and Wilbur Wright successfully fly a powered airplane

TESLA'S LIFE

1915

Sues Guglielmo Marconi over the use of his radio patents; gives first public description of "death ray"

1917

Receives Edison Medal

1909

Forms new company to make bladeless turbines

1910

1912

The *Titanic* sinks on its maiden voyage; more than 1,500 people die

1914

Archduke Franz Ferdinand is assassinated, launching World War I

1920

American women get the right to vote

WORLD EVENTS

1937

Discusses possible new defensive weapon later called the charged particle beam

1928

Receives last patent, for flying machine that combines features of a helicopter and a plane

1943

Dies January 7 in his rooms at the Hotel New Yorker

1940

1927

Charles Lindbergh makes the first solo nonstop transatlantic flight from New York to Paris

1936

African-American athlete Jesse Owens wins four gold medals at the Olympic Games in Berlin in the face of Nazi racial discrimination

1939

German troops invade Poland; Britain and France declare war on Germany; World War II (1939–1945) begins

DATE OF BIRTH: July 10, 1856

BIRTHPLACE: Smiljan, Austrian Croatia

FATHER: Milutin Tesla (1819–1879)

MOTHER: Djouka Mandic Tesla (1822–1892)

SIBLINGS: Dane, Angelina, Milka, Marica

DATE OF DEATH: January 7, 1943

PLACE OF BURIAL: Ashes originally kept in Ardsley-on-the-Hudson, New York; moved to the Nikola Tesla Museum in Belgrade in 1957

Further Reading

Aldrich, Lisa J. *Nikola Tesla and the Taming of Electricity.* Greensboro, N.C.: Morgan Reynolds Publishing, 2005.

Morgan, Sally. *Electricity and Electrical Circuits.* Chicago: Heinemann Library, 2008.

Ravage, Barbara. *George Westinghouse: A Genius for Invention.* Austin: Raintree Steck-Vaughn, 1997.

Rossi, Ann. *Bright Ideas: The Age of Invention in America, 1870–1910.* Washington, D.C.: National Geographic, 2005.

Stille, Darlene R. *Waves: Energy on the Move.* Minneapolis: Compass Point Books, 2006.

Look for more Signature Lives
books about this era:

Maya Angelou: *Poet, Performer, Activist*

George Washington Carver: *Scientist, Inventor, and Teacher*

Cesar Chavez: *Crusader for Social Change*

Hillary Rodham Clinton: *First Lady and Senator*

Amelia Earhart: *Legendary Aviator*

Thomas Alva Edison: *Great American Inventor*

Dolores Huerta: *Labor Leader and Civil Rights Activist*

Percy Lavon Julian: *Pioneering Chemist*

J. Pierpont Morgan: *Industrialist and Financier*

Alice Walker: *Author and Social Activist*

ON THE WEB

For more information on this topic,
use FactHound.
1. Go to *www.facthound.com*
2. Choose your grade level.
3. Begin your search.
The book's ID number is 9780756540869
FactHound will find the best
sites for you.

HISTORIC SITES

Nikola Tesla Statue
Niagara Falls, New York
Nikola Tesla Statue
Niagara Falls, Ontario, Canada
Monuments dedicated to Nikola Tesla near
Niagara Falls, where he helped build the
first AC hydroelectric power plant

U.S. Patent and Trademark Office Museum
600 Dulany St.
Alexandria, VA 22314
571/272-0095
Museum that showcases Americans'
inventive spirit

alternating current (AC)
electrical current that switches direction many times a second; this form of electricity is used in most buildings to power lights and appliances

direct current (DC)
electrical current that always moves in the same direction; this form of electricity is created by batteries and often used to power handheld devices

electromagnet
powerful magnet that temporarily gains an attractive force by an electrical current's passing through it

incandescent
emitting light as a result of a resistive filament's being heated to a high temperature

induction
process of moving electricity or magnetism between objects that aren't touching each other

insulated
protected from electric shock by materials that block the flow of electricity

patent
right to be the only one to make, use, or sell an invention for a certain number of years

physics
science that studies matter, energy, force, and motion

polarity
quality of having two oppositely charged poles, one positive and one negative

turbines
devices with curved blades connected to a central shaft that spins as speeding fluid (water or gas) passes over the blades

Source Notes

Chapter 1

Page 9, line 12: Nikola Tesla. *My Inventions*. New York: Beta Nu Publishing, 2007, p. 30.

Page 12, line 16: "Niagara Put in Harness." *The New York Times*. 7 July 1895, p. 20.

Page 12, line 26: Jill Jonnes. *Empires of Light: Edison, Tesla, Westinghouse, and the Race to Electrify the World*. New York: Random House, 2003, p. 326.

Page 13, line 11: Margaret Cheney and Robert Uth. *Tesla: Master of Lightning*. New York: Barnes and Noble Publishing, 1999, p. 80.

Chapter 2

Page 19, line 24: *My Inventions*, p. 19.

Page 21, line 7: Ibid., p. 27.

Page 21, line 22: *Tesla: Master of Lightning*, p. 4.

Page 23, line 3: *My Inventions*, p. 10.

Page 24, line 1: Ibid., p. 18.

Page 24, line 7: Nikola Tesla. "Some Personal Recollections." *Scientific American*. 5 June 1915. 5 Aug. 2008. http://www.rastko.org.yu/rastko/delo/10834

Page 25, line 12: *My Inventions*, p. 36.

Chapter 3

Page 28, line 7: Ibid., p. 38.

Page 30, line 9: Ibid., p. 40.

Page 31, line 10: Ibid., p. 20.

Page 32, line 28: Ibid., p. 42.

Page 33, line 11: Ibid., p. 43.

Chapter 4

Page 39, line 10: Mark J. Seifer. *Wizard: The Life and Times of Nikola Tesla*. New York: Citadel Press, 1998, p. 33.

Page 40, line 4: *My Inventions*, p. 50.

Page 41, line 2: "Tesla Says Edison Was an Empiricist." *The New York Times*. 19 Oct. 1931, p. 25.

Page 41, line 25: *My Inventions*, p. 51.

Page 43, line 1: Margaret Cheney. *Tesla: Man Out of Time*. New York: Touchstone, 1981, p. 55.

Page 43, line 7: "Some Personal Recollections."

Page 44, line 7: *Empires of Light: Edison, Tesla, Westinghouse, and the Race to Electrify the World*, p. 111.

Page 44, line 13: *Wizard: The Life and Times of Nikola Tesla*, p. 40.

Chapter 5

Page 50, line 3: Nikola Tesla. *The Essential Tesla: A New System of Alternating Current Motors and Transformers, Experiments with Alternate Currents of Very High Frequency*. Radford, Va.: Wilder Publications, 2007, p. 10.

Page 52, line 19: "Surer Than the Rope." *The New York Times*. 6 Dec. 1888, p. 5.

Page 53, line 6: "Far Worse Than Hanging." *The New York Times*. 7 Aug. 1890, p. 2.

Page 53, line 9: *Empires of Light: Edison, Tesla, Westinghouse, and the Race to Electrify the World*, p. 213.

Chapter 6

Page 61, line 1: Ibid., p. 232.

Page 61, line 10: *Wizard: The Life and Times of Nikola Tesla*, pp. 85, 88.

Page 61, line 21: *My Inventions*, p. 82.

Page 62, line 27: *Empires of Light: Edison, Tesla, Westinghouse, and the Race to Electrify the World*, p. 314.

Page 65, line 13: "Mr. Tesla's Great Loss." *The New York Times.* 14 March 1895, p. 9.

Chapter 7

Page 68, line 2: *Tesla: Man Out of Time*, p. 138.

Page 68, line 16: *My Inventions*, p. 85.

Page 70, line 7: Nikola Tesla. "The Problem of Increasing Human Energy." *Century Illustrated Magazine.* June 1900. 14 April 2008. www.tfcbooks.com/tesla/1900-06-00.htm

Page 73, line 8: *Wizard: The Life and Times of Nikola Tesla*, p. 256.

Page 75, line 13: "Poet and Visionary." Tesla: Master of Lightning. www.pbs.org/tesla/ll/ll_poevis.html. 15 April 2008.

Page 75, line 24: *Wizard: The Life and Times of Nikola Tesla*, p. 305.

Chapter 8

Page 77, line 9: *Tesla: Man Out of Time*, p. 215.

Page 79, line 12: "Tesla Sues Marconi on Wireless Patent." *The New York Times.* 4 Aug. 1915, p. 4.

Page 80, line 18: "Tesla's New Device Like Bolts of Thor." *The New York Times.* 8 Dec. 1915, p. 8.

Page 82, line 7: *Wizard: The Life and Times of Nikola Tesla*, p. 350.

Page 83, line 3: *Tesla: Man Out of Time*, p. 271.

Page 83, line 6: Nikola Tesla: Minutes of the Edison Medal Meeting, May 18, 1917, with Nikola Tesla's Acceptance Speech on Receiving the Edison Medal. www.rastko.org.yu/rastko/delo/10842. 25 Aug. 2008.

Page 83, line 27: *My Inventions*, pp. 78, 83.

Page 85, line 12: *Tesla: Man Out of Time*, p. 278.

Page 85, line 18: *Wizard: The Life and Times of Nikola Tesla*, p. 404.

Chapter 9

Page 87, line 9: Ibid., p. 416.

Page 87, line 13: *Tesla: Master of Lightning*, pp. 138–139.

Page 88, line 2: "Tesla at 75." *Time.* www.time.com/time/magazine/article/0,9171,742063-1,00.html. 16 April 2008.

Page 88, line 11: Ibid., www.time.com/time/magazine/article/0,9171,742063-3,00.html

Page 90, line 1: Nikola Tesla. "A Machine to End War." *Liberty.* February 1937. www.tfcbooks.com/tesla/1937-02-00.htm. 17 April 2008.

Page 92, line 15: William L. Laurence. "Science in the News." *The New York Times.* 22 Sept. 1940, p. D7.

Page 95, line 3: *My Inventions*, p. 67.

Cheney, Margaret. *Tesla: Man Out of Time*. New York: Touchstone, 1981.

Cheney, Margaret, and Robert Uth. *Tesla: Master of Lightning*. New York: Barnes and Noble Publishing, 1999.

Jonnes, Jill. *Empires of Light: Edison, Tesla, Westinghouse, and the Race to Electrify the World*. New York: Random House, 2003.

Mrkich, D. *Nikola Tesla: The European Years (1856–1884)*. Ottawa, Ontario: Commoners' Publishing, 2003. Reprinted, Serb National Federation. 1 April 2008. www.serbnatlfed.org/Archives/Tesla/tesla-ey.pdf

Nikola Tesla: Correspondence with Relatives. Trans. Nicholas Kosanovich. New York: Tesla Memorial Society Inc., 1995.

Seifer, Mark J. *Wizard: The Life and Times of Nikola Tesla*. New York: Citadel Press, 1998.

Svarney, Patricia, ed. The New York Public Library Science Desk Reference. New York: Macmillan, 1995.

Tesla, Nikola. *The Essential Tesla: A New System of Alternating Current Motors and Transformers, Experiments with Alternate Currents of Very High Frequency*. Radford, Va.: Wilder Publications, 2007.

Tesla, Nikola. My Inventions: The Autobiography of Nikola Tesla. New York: Beta Nu Publishing, 2007.

Tesla, Nikola. *My Inventions (An Autobiography)*. Internet Library of Serb Culture. 28 July 2008. www.rastko.org.yu/istorija/tesla/ntesla-autobiography.html

Tesla, Nikola. *"Some Personal Recollections." Scientific American*. 5 June 1915. 28 July 2008. www.rastko.org.yu/rastko/delo/10834

Michael Burgan is a freelance writer of books for children and adults. A history graduate of the University of Connecticut, he has written more than 100 fiction and nonfiction children's books. For adult audiences, he has written news articles, essays, and plays. Michael Burgan is a recipient of an Educational Press Association of America award.

Image Credits